EXPLORE!

FORCE OF NATURE

BLIZZARDS

BY MONIKA DAVIES

Please visit our website, www.enslow.com. For a free color catalog of all our high-quality books, call toll free 1-800-398-2504 or fax 1-877-980-4454.

Library of Congress Cataloging-in-Publication Data

Names: Davies, Monika, author.
Title: Blizzards / Monika Davies.
Description: New York : Enslow Publishing, [2021] | Series: Force of nature | Includes bibliographical references and index.
Identifiers: LCCN 2019045215 | ISBN 9781978518377 (library binding) | ISBN 9781978518360 (paperback) | ISBN 9781978518384 (ebook)
Subjects: LCSH: Blizzards—Juvenile literature.
Classification: LCC QC926.32 .D38 2021 | DDC 551.55/5—dc23
LC record available at https://lccn.loc.gov/2019045215

Published in 2021 by
Enslow Publishing
101 West 23rd Street, Suite #240
New York, NY 10011

Copyright © 2021 Enslow Publishing

Designer: Katelyn E. Reynolds
Editor: Monika Davies

Photo credits: Cover, p. 1 John Normile/Getty Images; cover, pp. 1–48 (series art) Merfin/Shutterstock.com; pp. 4, 31, 37 courtesy of NOAA; p. 5 blvdone/Shutterstock.com; p. 6 KLH49/iStock/Getty Images Plus; p. 7 Vladimir_Sotnichenko/Shutterstock.com; p. 8 Bobkov Evgeniy/Shutterstock.com; p. 9 Artisticco/Shutterstock.com; p. 10 Ryan W Brown/Moment/Getty Images; p. 11 (main) Haywiremedia/Shutterstock.com; p. 11 (inset) Titova Iuliia/Shutterstock.com; p. 12 justoomm/Shutterstock.com; p. 13 vm/E+/Getty Images; p. 14 Avatar_023/Shutterstock.com; p. 15 GOPEN RAI/AFP/Getty Images; p. 16 Herbert A. French/Buyenlarge/Getty Images; pp. 17, 19 Bettmann/Getty Images; p. 18 Underwood Archives/Getty Images; p. 20 Metilsteiner/Wikipedia.org; p. 21 Wallace G. Levison/Dahlstrom Collection/The LIFE Picture Collection via Getty Images; pp. 22, 24, 25 courtesy of SUNY Buffalo State Archives, _Courier-express_Collection; p. 23 Rainer Lesniewski/Shutterstock.com; p. 27 Robert Rosamilio/NY Daily News Archive via Getty Images; pp. 28, 30 Bill Turnbull/NY Daily News Archive via Getty Images; p. 29 Harry Hamburg/NY Daily News Archive via Getty Images; pp. 32, 38 courtesy of NASA; p. 33 JEWEL SAMAD/AFP/Getty Images; p. 34 USGS/NASA Earth Observatory/Joshua Stevens/Mike Carlowicz; p. 35 eddtoro/Shutterstock.com; p. 39 courtesy of the Joint Polar Satellite System/NOAA; p. 40 Upstate Amanda/Shutterstock.com; p. 41 Benjamin C. Tankersley/For the Washington Post via Getty Images; p. 42 © iStockphoto.com/JulNichols; p. 43 Alan Budman/Shutterstock.com; p. 44 Barry Chin/The Boston Globe via Getty Images; p. 45 m.czosnek/iStock/Getty Images Plus.

Portions of this work were originally authored by Michael Portman and published as _Blinding Blizzards_. All new material in this edition was authored by Monika Davies.

All rights reserved. No part of this book may be reproduced in any form without permission in writing from the publisher, except by a reviewer.

Printed in the United States of America

Some of the images in this book illustrate individuals who are models. The depictions do not imply actual situations or events.

CPSIA compliance information: Batch #BS20ENS: For further information contact Enslow Publishing, New York, New York, at 1-800-542-2595.

CONTENTS

Blinding Blizzards 4

The Backstory of Blizzards 6

History-Making Blizzards 16

The Storm of the Century 26

Preparing for the Future 36

Glossary 46

For More Information 47

Index 48

WORDS IN THE GLOSSARY APPEAR IN **BOLD** TYPE THE FIRST TIME THEY ARE USED IN THE TEXT.

BLINDING BLIZZARDS

When the sun disappears and the sky turns into a blinding blanket of white snow, you can bet you're headed into a blizzard! Blizzards are storms of epic proportions, characterized by a high quantity of blowing snow and strong, fast winds. These storms are forces of nature, often responsible for power outages, property **damage**, and sometimes multiple **casualties**.

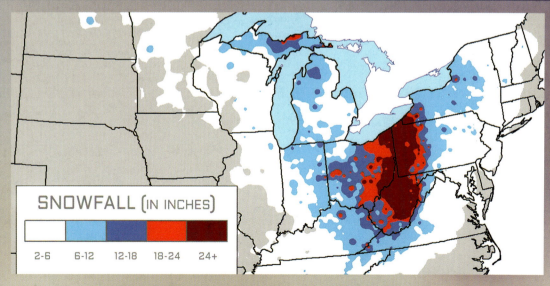

SNOWFALL (IN INCHES)
2-6 | 6-12 | 12-18 | 18-24 | 24+

IN NOVEMBER 1950, THE GREAT APPALACHIAN STORM RAGED THROUGH EASTERN AMERICA, DUMPING OVER 30 INCHES (76 CM) OF SNOW IN AREAS FROM NORTH CAROLINA TO OHIO AND WEST VIRGINIA.

WINTER STORM JONAS, NEW YORK CITY

The United States has seen its fair share of blizzards, from the Great Blizzard of 1888 to Winter Storm Jonas of 2016. In this book, we'll examine the makings of a blizzard, a few **extreme** blizzards throughout American history, and how we can prepare for the blizzards of the future.

THE BACKSTORY OF BLIZZARDS

According to the U.S. National Weather Service (NWS), a blizzard is a storm that lasts at least three hours and includes large amounts of falling or blowing snow. Blizzard winds are faster than 35 miles (56 km) per hour, and visibility is less than 1/4 mile (0.4 km). A severe blizzard is one with temperatures below 10°F (−12°C), winds above 45 miles (72 km) per hour, and visibility near zero.

THE WORD "BLIZZARD" ORIGINALLY MEANT A LARGE AMOUNT OF GUNFIRE. IN THE 1870S, A NEWSPAPER IN IOWA USED BLIZZARD TO DESCRIBE A SNOWSTORM. SOON, BLIZZARD BECAME THE COMMON TERM FOR A MAJOR SNOWSTORM.

VISIBILITY:
THE ABILITY TO SEE OR BE SEEN

EXPLORE MORE

NOT ALL SNOWSTORMS ARE BLIZZARDS. AND NOT ALL BLIZZARDS ARE ACCOMPANIED BY FALLING SNOW. SOMETIMES, STRONG WINDS BLOW AROUND SNOW THAT HAS ALREADY FALLEN, CREATING A BLIZZARD. THE BLOWING SNOW CAUSES THE SAME BLINDING, UNSAFE CONDITIONS AS FALLING SNOW.

All air contains **water vapor**. When air rises into the upper atmosphere, it cools. The water vapor begins to change into tiny drops of water, which collect around bits of dust. Water drops and dust are what clouds are made of. As the temperature in the cloud dips several degrees below freezing, the small water drops turn into tiny ice crystals. These ice crystals stick together until they form snowflakes.

SNOW AND WATER

When snowflakes get bigger, they become heavier and fall out of the clouds. If the air gets warmer as the snowflakes fall, they melt and turn into rain. If the air stays cold, the snowflakes fall to the ground as snow. Different types of snow contain different amounts of water. For example, if you melted 10 inches (25 cm) of snow, it could result in anywhere from less than an inch (2.5 cm) to as much as 3 inches (7.6 cm) of liquid water. Generally, the colder the air temperature and ground temperature, the drier the snow will be.

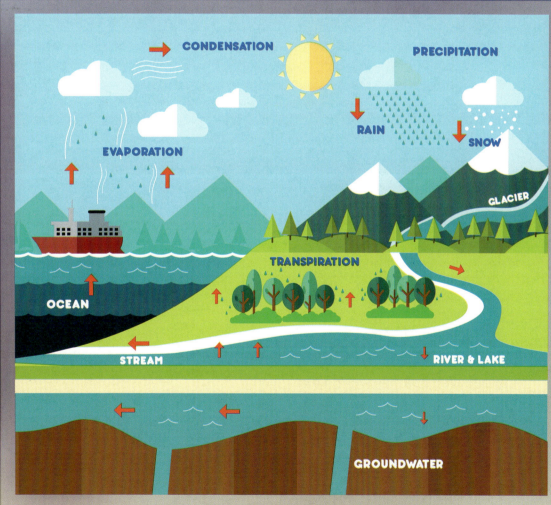

SNOWFALL IS PART OF THE WATER CYCLE, OR THE MODEL SCIENTISTS USE TO SHOW HOW WATER MOVES BETWEEN EARTH, UNDERGROUND, AND THE ATMOSPHERE.

It takes only a little snow to create problems in cities and towns, especially in places where snowfall is uncommon. Blizzards make these problems add up quickly. Strong winds can turn powdery snow into a whiteout, making it hard to see. Whiteouts, along with snowdrifts, make traveling by car or airplane unsafe and sometimes impossible.

DRIVING DURING A SNOWSTORM CAN QUICKLY BECOME DANGEROUS IF THE WIND PICKS UP OR A LOT OF SNOW BUILDS UP ON THE ROADS.

HEAVY, WET SNOW CAN WEIGH DOWN ROOFS OF BUILDINGS, CAUSING THEM TO CAVE IN. STRONG WINDS AND HEAVY SNOW CAN BREAK TREE LIMBS AND POWER LINES. THE EXTREME COLD TEMPERATURES THAT ACCOMPANY BLIZZARDS CAN ALSO MAKE WATER PIPES FREEZE OR BURST.

WHITEOUT: A CONDITION IN WHICH FALLING OR BLOWING SNOW MAKES VISIBILITY VERY POOR

EXPLORE MORE

IT'S POSSIBLE FOR SNOW TO FALL ON A MOUNTAINTOP WHILE IT'S WARM, RAINING, OR EVEN SUNNY IN A VALLEY BELOW. THIS IS BECAUSE THE AIR AT THE TOP OF THE MOUNTAIN IS MUCH COLDER THAN THE AIR IN THE VALLEY.

SNOW IN THE HIMALAYAS

During a blizzard, strong winds can make the air temperature feel much colder than it actually is. This is called windchill. For instance, a wind that's 35 miles (56 km) per hour combined with a temperature of 30°F (−1°C) can feel like 14°F (−10°C).

Another danger of windchill is hypothermia. This occurs when the body loses heat faster than it can produce it. Cold wind can reduce body heat very quickly. Normally, body temperature is around 98.6°F (37°C). Hypothermia causes a person's body temperature to drop below 95°F (35°C). As the body cools, the heart, lungs, and other organs stop working properly. If left untreated, hypothermia can lead to death.

IF A BLIZZARD IS RAGING OUTSIDE, IT'S BEST TO STAY INSIDE AND KEEP WARM.

RECOGNIZING HYPOTHERMIA

It's incredibly important to recognize the signs of hypothermia, especially for people who are very young or elderly. Signs of hypothermia include uncontrollable shivering and confusion. A person may also have trouble speaking and moving. Another sign of hypothermia is a lack of energy. Someone who is very sleepy may be suffering from hypothermia. To treat hypothermia, people should be moved to a warm location. Wet clothing should then be removed. It's critical to warm the center of the body first, not the arms and legs. Someone suffering from hypothermia should drink warm liquids and seek medical attention as soon as possible.

HYPOTHERMIA IS AN EMERGENCY. IF SOMEONE YOU KNOW IS SHOWING THE SIGNS OF HYPOTHERMIA, CALL 911!

WINDCHILL:
THE EFFECT THAT WIND HAS OF CAUSING AIR TO FEEL COLDER THAN IT IS

SIGNS OF FROSTBITE

 COLD, BURNING, PAINFUL, OR ITCHY SKIN

 LOSS OF FEELING, ESPECIALLY IN FINGERS, TOES, EARS, NOSE, OR CHIN

 PALE OR WHITE APPEARANCE IN AREAS EXPOSED TO EXTREME COLD

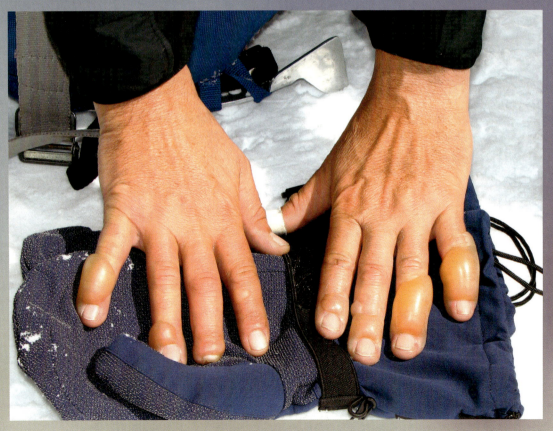

 PEOPLE EXPOSED TO EXTREMELY LOW WINDCHILL TEMPERATURES FACE THE DANGER OF FROSTBITE. FROSTBITE OCCURS WHEN SKIN OR CELLS BENEATH THE SKIN FREEZE. FROSTBITE CAN CAUSE LASTING DAMAGE.

DEPENDING ON THE TEMPERATURE AND WIND SPEED OUTSIDE, IT CAN TAKE AROUND 5 TO 30 MINUTES OF OUTSIDE EXPOSURE TO LEAD TO FROSTBITE.

TREATMENTS

 SOAK FROSTBITTEN AREAS IN WARM WATER

 DON'T RUB FROSTBITTEN BODY PARTS OR EXPOSE THEM TO DIRECT HEAT, SUCH AS STOVES, FIREPLACES, OR HEATING PADS

 SEEK MEDICAL ATTENTION AS SOON AS POSSIBLE

HISTORY-MAKING BLIZZARDS

March 1888 began with unusually warm temperatures along the East Coast of the United States. However, on March 12, temperatures dropped. The warm rain started to freeze, and the wind began to howl. By midnight, the rain had turned into snow.

For almost two days, snow and wind continued nonstop. By the time the storm ended, between 40 and 50 inches (102 and 127 cm) of snow had fallen in many places. Major cities, including New York City and Boston, Massachusetts, were at a standstill.

THE GREAT BLIZZARD OF 1888 IS ALSO KNOWN IN HISTORY AS THE GREAT WHITE **HURRICANE** BECAUSE OF ITS SIZE AND DESTRUCTION. IT'S ONE OF THE MOST FAMOUS STORMS IN AMERICAN HISTORY.

NEW YORK CITY, MARCH 1888

FREEZE:
TO BECOME A SOLID, SUCH AS ICE, BECAUSE OF COLD

The strong winds of the 1888 storm snapped **telegraph** and telephone wires, and snow blocked roads and railways. In some areas, the heavy winds created **snowdrifts** 50 feet (15 m) high! Trains were either stopped or took hours to travel just a few miles. In New York City, people climbed down from a stuck elevated train using ladders. In the end, more than 400 people died as a result of the Great Blizzard of 1888.

NORTHAMPTON, MASSACHUSETTS, MARCH 14, 1888

THE BLIZZARD OF 1888 CAUSED ELECTRICAL POLES AND WIRES TO FALL. THIS CAUSED EVEN MORE DANGEROUS CONDITIONS FOR THOSE LIVING IN NEW YORK CITY.

EXPLORE MORE

DURING THE 1888 STORM, WIND SPEEDS EXCEEDED 60 MILES (97 KM) PER HOUR. GUSTS OF OVER 80 MILES (129 KM) PER HOUR WERE REPORTED ON LONG ISLAND, NEW YORK. THE WINDS AND FALLING SNOW ERASED FOOTPRINTS IN LESS THAN FIVE MINUTES!

GUST:
A SUDDEN, POWERFUL WIND

GOING UNDERGROUND

The Great Blizzard of 1888 led to the creation of the New York City Subway, an underground railway system. Trains on ground tracks and those that were elevated had been useless during the blizzard. City officials saw the need to take transportation underground and started planning for an underground subway system. In 1904, the New York Subway officially began operating. Telegraph and power wires also snapped during the storm, prompting officials to decide to move power lines underground. This way, power would not be lost during a similar storm.

THE BLIZZARD OF MARCH 11TH, 12TH, AND 13TH, 1888.
PHOTOGRAPHS TAKEN JUST AFTER THE STORM, BY LANGILL.

THE *NEW YORK TIMES* STATED ON MARCH 13, 1888, THAT THE GREAT WHITE HURRICANE "**ISOLATED** THE CITY FROM THE REST OF THE COUNTRY, CAUSED MANY ACCIDENTS AND GREAT DISCOMFORT AND EXPOSED IT TO MANY DANGERS."

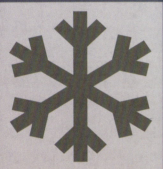

EXPLORE MORE

DURING THE GREAT BLIZZARD OF 1888, PEOPLE TRIED TO MELT THE MOUNDS OF SNOW BY SETTING FIRES. FIRES THAT GOT OUT OF CONTROL DID GREAT DAMAGE TO BUILDINGS SINCE FIREFIGHTERS COULDN'T RESPOND QUICKLY ENOUGH.

BROOKLYN BRIDGE, MARCH 14, 1888

The Blizzard of 1977 is the most famous blizzard in the history of Buffalo, New York. The winter of 1976 to 1977 had been especially bitter. Snow that had fallen throughout November, December, and January never had a chance to melt.

January 28, 1977, started out as a calm, mild day. Overnight, the temperature had risen to 26°F (−3°C). But just before noon, cold air moved in. Within a few hours, the temperature plunged to 0°F (−18°C), while the wind blew over 45 miles (72 km) per hour. Strong gusts dropped the windchill to −60°F (−51°C).

THE BLIZZARD HIT BEFORE THE TIME OF COMPUTERS, INSTANT MESSAGING, AND SMARTPHONES. METEOROLOGISTS FOUND OUT A MASSIVE STORM WAS ROLLING IN LATE THE FIRST MORNING, AND MANY PEOPLE HAD ALREADY GONE TO WORK BEFORE THEY COULD BE INFORMED.

METEOROLOGIST:
A SCIENTIST WHO STUDIES THE ATMOSPHERE AND WEATHER

THE BLIZZARD OF 1977 HIT WESTERN NEW YORK STATE AS WELL AS SOUTHERN ONTARIO, CANADA.

During the next few days, only about 12 inches (30 cm) of new snow fell. However, the snow that had piled up on frozen Lake Erie continued to blow into Buffalo and the surrounding areas. Snowdrifts were so high that some houses were buried up to the roofs. Thousands of cars were abandoned in the streets, completely covered with snow.

ON THE FIRST DAY OF FEBRUARY, THE BLIZZARD OF 1977 CAME TO AN END. CLEANUP, HOWEVER, CONTINUED THROUGHOUT THE REST OF THE MONTH AND COST OVER $20 MILLION.

SNOWY RECORDS

The Blizzard of 1977 sealed Buffalo's standing as one of the snowiest cities in the United States. Buffalo usually receives around 97 inches (246 cm) of snow per year. In 1977, Buffalo received 199.4 inches (506.5 cm) of snow. The Blizzard of 1977 was also the first blizzard in U.S. history to be declared a national **disaster**. Over 500 people from the U.S. National Guard and about 300 U.S. Army soldiers were part of the task force to clear snow and rescue people. Twenty-nine people lost their lives during the storm, including nine people who were trapped in their cars.

DURING THE BLIZZARD OF 1977, BLOCKED ROADS PREVENTED SNOWPLOWS FROM CLEARING THE SNOW. TRAVEL INTO AND OUT OF BUFFALO WAS NEARLY IMPOSSIBLE.

THE STORM OF THE CENTURY

In March 1993, three different storm systems combined in the Gulf of Mexico to create a giant storm that some people call the "Storm of the Century" or the "Superstorm of 1993." For several days, snow fell as far south as Florida and as far north as Canada.

The storm affected tens of millions of people on the East Coast of North America. According to a senior meteorologist at AccuWeather.com, "The storm produced an extremely rare, massive swath of 1- to 3-foot [30 to 91 cm] snowfall. When combined with wind gusts of tropical storm to hurricane force, it brought snowdrifts as high as single-story homes to the Appalachians."

A SENIOR METEOROLOGIST AT ACCUWEATHER.COM STATED, "THE BLIZZARD OF '93 IS A GOOD EXAMPLE OF A 'SNOWICANE.' IT WAS THE GRANDDADDY OF 'EM ALL."

SWATH:
A LONG, WIDE BAND OF SOMETHING

27

During the storm, winds sometimes gusted over 100 miles (160 km) an hour. Major airports were shut down. Birmingham, Alabama, a city that normally gets less than 2 inches (5 cm) of snow per year, received 13 inches (33 cm) of snow during the storm. As a result of the storm, a ship called the *Gold Bond Conveyor* sank in the Atlantic Ocean. The storm system also brought thunderstorms, floods, and windstorms to other parts of the country.

WHEN A BIG STORM LIKE A BLIZZARD IS ABOUT TO HIT, MANY PEOPLE STOCK UP ON WATER, BREAD, MILK, AND OTHER FOODS. HOWEVER, SOMETIMES, STORMS COME IN TOO FAST, AND THERE'S NO TIME.

MANY TRAVELERS WERE UNABLE TO GET WHERE THEY WANTED TO GO DURING THE SUPERSTORM OF 1993, SUCH AS THOSE SHOWN HERE AT PENN STATION IN NEW YORK CITY.

EXPLORE MORE

THE STORM OF THE CENTURY DUMPED HEAPS OF SNOW ON SEVERAL CITIES. MOUNT LECONTE, TENNESSEE, RECEIVED 56 INCHES (142 CM), WHILE 50 INCHES (127 CM) FELL IN MOUNT MITCHELL, NORTH CAROLINA.

In total, over $6 billion in damage was caused by the blizzard. The storm ended up hitting 26 states and a large portion of eastern Canada. By the end of the storm, it was **estimated** the blizzard was responsible for over 300 deaths.

The storm took a costly and devastating toll on the U.S. East Coast. However, the damage could have been much worse. The National Weather Service was able to predict the storm five days in advance and the blizzard conditions two days before. Over 100 million people were able to prepare for the storm before it struck.

IN NEW YORK CITY, THE STORM HAD SNOW REMOVAL TEAMS OUT IN FULL FORCE. OVER 1,200 SNOWPLOWS AND AROUND 350 SALT SPREADERS CAME OUT IN AN EFFORT TO KEEP THE STREETS CLEAR AND SAFE.

DEVASTATING:
CAUSING WIDESPREAD DAMAGE

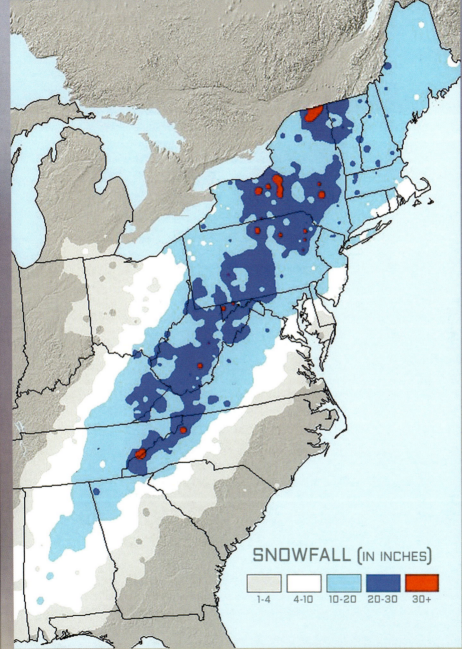

SNOWFALL (IN INCHES)

1-4　4-10　10-20　20-30　30+

THIS IMAGE SHOWS THE AMOUNT OF SNOW THAT FELL IN DIFFERENT AREAS OF THE U.S. EAST COAST BETWEEN MARCH 12 AND MARCH 14, 1993.

EXPLORE MORE

USING COMPUTER MODELS, THE NATIONAL WEATHER SERVICE WAS ABLE TO PREDICT THE UPCOMING "STORM OF THE CENTURY" AND SENT OUT A SEVERE STORM WARNING. THIS GAVE STATE GOVERNORS THE OPPORTUNITY TO DECLARE A STATE OF EMERGENCY, GIVING MILLIONS OF PEOPLE TIME TO PREPARE.

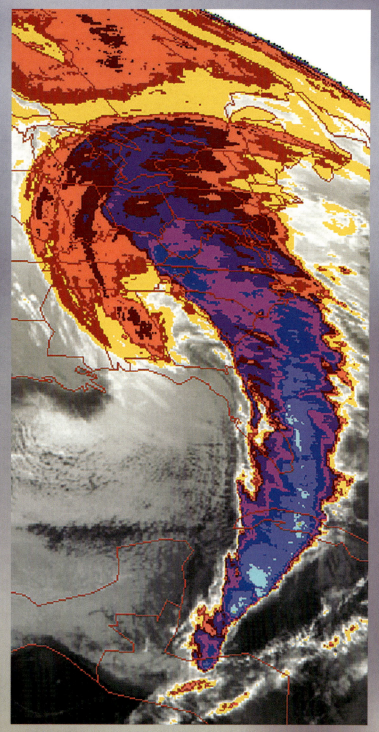

THIS IS A NASA SATELLITE IMAGE OF THE MARCH 1993 BLIZZARD. ACCORDING TO A WRITER AT THE *NEW YORK TIMES*, THE STORM OF MARCH 1993 WAS "A MONSTER WITH THE HEART OF A BLIZZARD AND THE SOUL OF A HURRICANE."

SNOWMAGEDDON

For residents on the northeast coast of America, the winter of 2010 was a stormy one. In February 2010, two snowstorms stormed through this area of the United States, dumping record amounts of snow. The first blizzard blew through from February 5 to 6, dumping 17.8 inches (45.2 cm) of snow on Washington, DC. This blustery blizzard earned the nickname "Snowmageddon" or "Snowpocalypse." The second storm swept through from February 9 to 10, blanketing Washington, DC, with 10.8 inches (27.4 cm) of snow. The city's total snowfall for the month totaled 32.1 inches (81.5 cm). This was almost seven times the amount of snow the city normally gets in a month!

SILVER SPRING, MARYLAND, FEBRUARY 6, 2010

WINTER STORM JONAS

From January 22 to 24, 2016, Winter Storm Jonas wreaked **havoc** on the East Coast. Dumping over 30 inches (76 cm) of snow on several cities, the storm prompted some changes in its aftermath. Jonas snowed on the Pennsylvania Turnpike, a toll highway, and backed up traffic for hours. Over 500 cars, trucks, and buses were caught on the highway, unable to move during the storm. Following an **evaluation** of the state's response to the storm, there are now stockpiles within close distance of the entire stretch of highway. These stockpiles include bottles of water, food, blankets, and more items to help out if another blizzard hits.

THIS IS AN AERIAL VIEW OF VIRGINIA, MARYLAND, AND WASHINGTON, DC, PHOTOGRAPHED ON JANUARY 24, 2016. AROUND 18 TO 24 INCHES (46 TO 61 CM) OF SNOW FELL ON THESE AREAS DURING WINTER STORM JONAS. THE WHITE COLOR IN THIS PHOTO SHOWS WHERE THE SNOW FELL!

BRONX, NEW YORK, JANUARY 23, 2016

AFTERMATH:
THE PERIOD OF TIME FOLLOWING A DEVASTATING EVENT

PREPARING FOR THE FUTURE

Today, computer programs are used to predict the path that a blizzard might take. These programs use facts gathered from radar, satellites, and radiosondes in order to create models of a storm system.

Radar towers contain machines that use radio waves to locate and identify objects. Radar machines were first used to spot aircraft during World War II. A radar tower can monitor different types of **precipitation** and which way clouds are turning, as well as wind strength. Radar towers are also useful when tracking the direction of a storm.

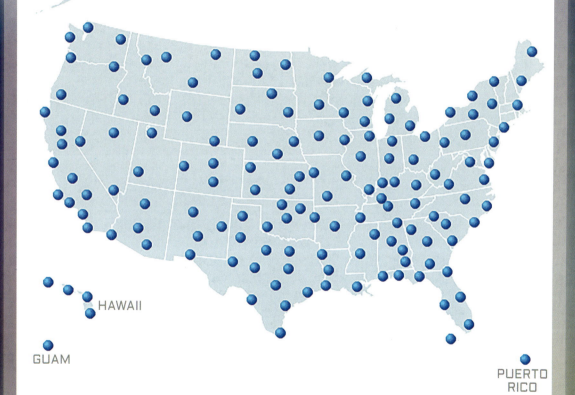

● NWS/DoD RADAR SITES

THIS MAP SHOWS THE LOCATIONS OF THE RADAR TOWERS RUN BY THE NATIONAL OCEANIC AND ATMOSPHERIC ADMINISTRATION (NOAA) THROUGHOUT THE UNITED STATES.

Satellites orbiting Earth also gather useful data for predicting storms. Pictures taken by satellites can show a storm as it's forming as well as track its movement.

Radiosondes are instruments that provide upper-air data. These instruments are attached to weather balloons and send back measurements using radio signals. Radiosondes take measurements of temperature, wind speed, and water vapor levels.

SATELLITE:
AN OBJECT THAT CIRCLES EARTH IN ORDER TO COLLECT AND SEND INFORMATION OR AID IN COMMUNICATION

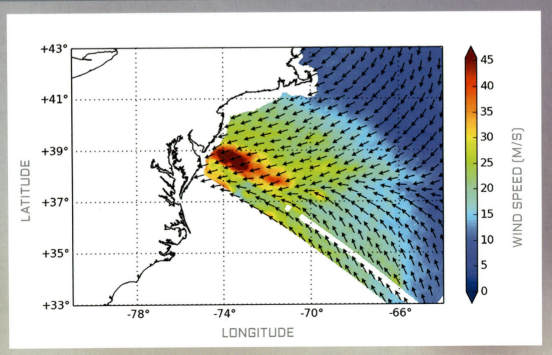

THIS GRAPH SHOWS RAPIDSCAT DATA FOR WINTER STORM JONAS. THE RAPIDSCAT INSTRUMENT TRACKS AND MEASURES SURFACE WINDS OVER THE OCEAN FROM ITS PERCH ON THE INTERNATIONAL SPACE STATION (ISS).

OBSERVING EARTH

NOAA has three types of satellites that provide data for weather forecasts. Polar orbiting satellites circle Earth around 520 miles (840 km) above the surface. These satellites capture six or seven pictures of Earth every day, showing how the weather looks around the world. Geostationary satellites hover over the same spot on Earth every day and are stationed far, far away. These satellites are located around 22,300 miles (35,800 km) above Earth's surface! They take photos of the whole Earth. Deep space satellites are directed toward the sun. These satellites are tracking solar storms, as well as space weather.

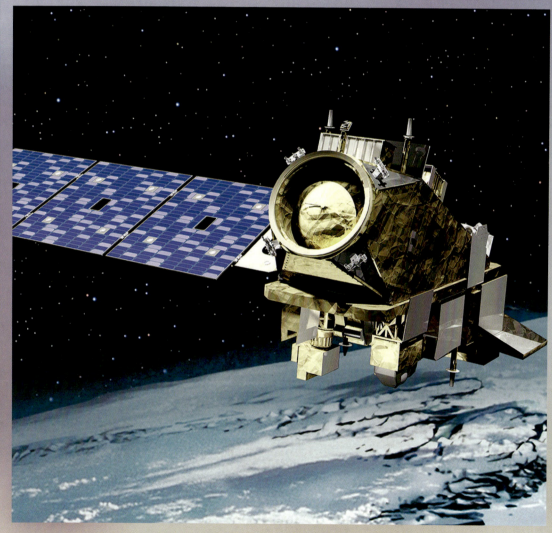

NOAA AND NASA (NATIONAL AERONAUTICS AND SPACE ADMINISTRATION) ARE WORKING TOGETHER ON SATELLITES AND SPACECRAFT THAT CAN HELP MAKE WEATHER PREDICTION BETTER.

When all of these methods are combined, forecasters can often predict when and where a blizzard will strike. However, even areas that know a blizzard is coming are often unprepared or unable to deal with the storm. During blizzards across the United States, there are still cases of people getting stuck underground in subways or stranded in their cars on highways.

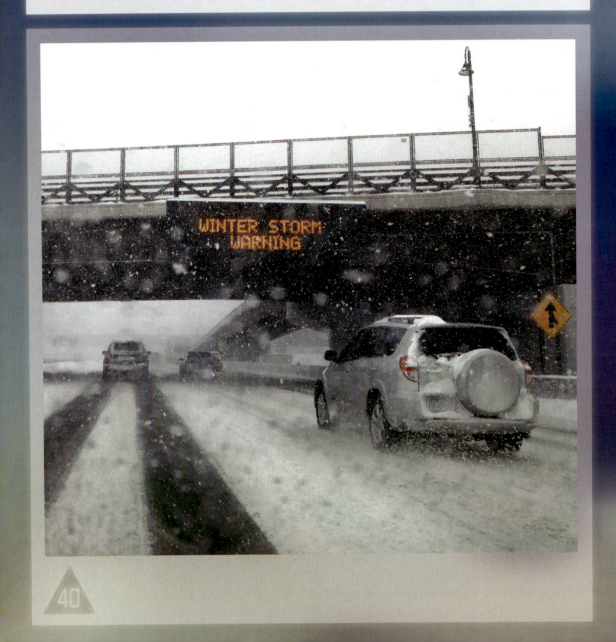

IF THE WEATHER STARTS TO BECOME MORE SEVERE, FORECASTERS WILL RELEASE WEATHER BALLOONS INTO THE AIR MORE OFTEN IN ORDER TO COLLECT FURTHER DATA ABOUT STORM CONDITIONS.

EXPLORE MORE

THE NOAA ALSO USES ITS WEATHER AND CLIMATE OPERATIONAL SUPERCOMPUTER SYSTEM TO HELP PREDICT WEATHER PATTERNS. THESE SUPERCOMPUTERS COMPLETE CALCULATIONS THAT HELP FORECAST WEATHER. THEY USE DATA FROM RADAR TOWERS, RADIOSONDES, SATELLITES, AND OTHER INSTRUMENTS.

If a person is caught in a blizzard, the most important thing they can do is find refuge and stay dry. Hypothermia and frostbite can occur very quickly if a person gets wet in the cold. During winter, it's a good idea to keep blankets, flashlights, and snacks in the car in case the car gets stuck in a storm.

Blizzards can be devastating storms, piling up streets with snow and bringing an entire city to a standstill. However, with our current forecasting technology, it's easier to predict when and where a blizzard will strike. Forces of nature do bring their own set of risks and dangers, but with preparation, we can ready ourselves to face these storms.

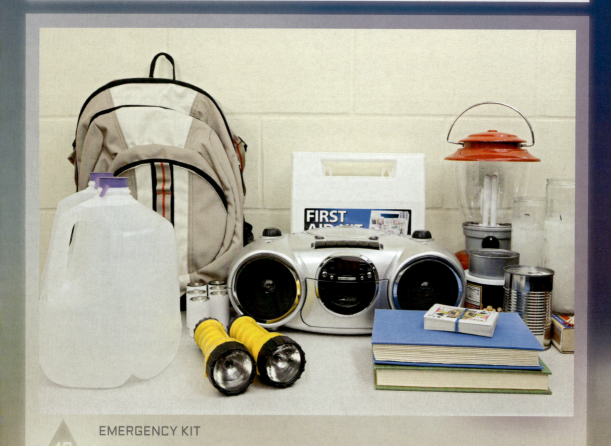

EMERGENCY KIT

REFUGE:
SHELTER FROM DANGER

BLIZZARDS CAN APPEAR TERRIFYING. HOWEVER, WE CAN LISTEN TO EMERGENCY ALERTS AND FOLLOW SAFETY INSTRUCTIONS FROM CITY OFFICIALS TO STAY SAFE DURING AN **INTENSE** STORM.

EXPLORE MORE

YOU CAN STAY UP-TO-DATE ON A STORM WITH EMERGENCY ALERTS FROM THE NATIONAL EMERGENCY ALERT SYSTEM (EAS) OR BY LISTENING TO THE NOAA WEATHER RADIO. BOTH PROVIDE INFORMATION AND WARNINGS ABOUT POTENTIAL STORM HAZARDS.

43

THE EFFECTS OF CLIMATE CHANGE

Climate change has directly led to an increase in global temperatures. Climate change has led to ocean surface temperatures increasing. This, in turn, has led to more moisture flowing into Earth's atmosphere. Remember, heavy snowfall is caused by two elements. First, temperatures must be cold enough for snow to fall. Second, Earth's atmosphere must be wet, or moist. More moisture in the atmosphere can equal heavier snowfall. This can directly lead to more intense blizzards. Some experts believe that climate change may lead to shorter winter seasons but more forceful blizzards.

BLIZZARDS CAN CAUSE HOMES TO ABRUPTLY LOSE POWER AND HEAT. THIS MEANS IT'S ALSO A GOOD IDEA TO KEEP YOUR HOUSE STOCKED WITH FLASHLIGHTS, A BATTERY-POWERED RADIO, AND FOOD THAT DOESN'T NEED TO BE COOKED.

SPECIALLY TRAINED CREWS FIX POWER LINES DOWNED BY STORMS. BUT, SOMETIMES STORMS PREVENT CREWS FROM BEING ABLE TO DO THE WORK RIGHT AWAY.

CLIMATE CHANGE:
THE LONG-TERM CHANGE IN EARTH'S CLIMATE, CAUSED PARTLY BY HUMAN ACTIVITIES SUCH AS BURNING OIL AND NATURAL GAS

GLOSSARY

casualty A person who gets hurt or dies in an event.

damage Harm; also, to cause harm.

disaster An event that causes much suffering or loss.

estimate To make a careful guess about an answer based on the known facts.

evaluation The act of determining the condition of something.

extreme Great or severe.

havoc Circumstances where there is much destruction.

hurricane A powerful storm that forms over water and causes heavy rainfall and high winds.

intense Existing in an extreme degree.

isolate To keep apart from others.

precipitation Rain, snow, sleet, or hail.

snowdrift A mound of snow created by wind.

telegraph A method of communicating using electric signals sent through wires.

water vapor Water in the form of gas.

FOR MORE INFORMATION

BOOKS

DK Publishing. *Eyewitness Weather*. New York, NY: DK Publishing, 2016.

Duey, Kathleen, and Karen A. Bale. *Blizzard: Colorado, 1886*. New York, NY: Aladdin, 2014.

Kostigen, Thomas. *Extreme Weather: Surviving Tornadoes, Sandstorms, Hailstorms, Blizzards, Hurricanes, and More!* Washington, DC: National Geographic, 2014.

Tarshis, Lauren. *I Survived the Children's Blizzard, 1888*. New York, NY: Scholastic Press, 2018.

WEBSITES

The 11 Worst Blizzards in U.S. History
www.thoughtco.com/worst-blizzards-in-american-history-1140776
Discover more facts about some of the worst blizzards in American history.

What Is a Ground Blizzard?
www.weather.gov/safety/winter-ground-blizzard
Learn more about ground blizzards and how to stay safe in a blizzard on this website.

Winter Storms Are Different!
eo.ucar.edu/kids/dangerwx/blizzard1.htm
Test your blizzard knowledge and learn more about how blizzards form.

Publisher's note to educators and parents: Our editors have carefully reviewed these websites to ensure that they are suitable for students. Many websites change frequently, however, and we cannot guarantee that a site's future contents will continue to meet our high standards of quality and educational value. Be advised that students should be closely supervised whenever they access the internet.

INDEX

B
Blizzard of 1977, 22–24, 25
Buffalo, NY, 22, 24, 25

C
casualties/deaths, 4, 18, 25, 30
climate change, 44

F
frostbite, 14, 15, 42

G
Gold Bond Conveyor, 28
Great Blizzard of 1888, 5, 16–18, 19, 20, 21

H
hypothermia, 12, 13, 42

N
National Emergency Alert System (EAS), 43
National Oceanic and Atmospheric Administration (NOAA), 39, 41, 43
New York City, 16, 18, 20
New York Subway, 20

R
radar, 36, 41
radiosondes, 36, 38, 41

S
satellites, 36, 38, 39, 41
snowdrifts, 10, 18, 24, 25
Snowmageddon (2010), 33
Storm of the Century (1993), 26–30, 32

T
temperatures, 6, 8, 9, 12, 16, 22, 38, 44

U
U.S. National Weather Service (NWS), 6, 30, 32

V
visibility, 6, 10

W
Washington, DC, 33
water vapor, 8, 38
weather balloons, 38
whiteouts, 10
wind/wind speed, 4, 6, 7, 10, 12, 16, 18, 19, 22, 26, 28, 36, 38
windchill, 12, 22
Winter Storm Jonas, 5, 34